foundations
SMALL GROUP STUDY

taught by tom Holladay and kay warren

THE BIBLE

SADDLEBACK CHURCH

ZONDERVAN.com/
AUTHORTRACKER
follow your favorite authors

Foundations: *The Bible Study Guide*
Copyright © 2003, 2008 by Tom Holladay and Kay Warren

Requests for information should be addressed to:
Zondervan, *Grand Rapids, Michigan* 49530

ISBN 978-0-310-27670-8

08 09 10 11 12 13 14 15 16 17 18 • 23 22 21 20 19 18 17 16 15 14 13 12 11 10 9 8 7 6 5 4 3 2 1

Small Group Roster .... Inside Front Cover

Foreword *by Rick Warren* iv

Preface vi

How to Use This Video Curriculum ix

Session One: Building Confidence in the Bible 1

Session Two: Trusting in the Reliability of the Bible 11

Session Three: Understanding Illumination 21

Session Four: Handling the Bible Responsibly 31

Small Group Resources 39

    Helps for Hosts 40

    Frequently Asked Questions 44

    Group Guidelines 46

    Circles of Life Diagram 48

    Small Group Prayer and Praise Report 49

    Small Group Calendar 52

    Answer Key 53

    Key Verses 55

FOREWORD

What *Foundations* Will Do for You

I once built a log cabin in the Sierra mountains of northern California. After ten backbreaking weeks of clearing forest land, all I had to show for my effort was a leveled and squared concrete foundation. I was discouraged, but my father, who built over a hundred church buildings in his lifetime, said, "Cheer up, son! Once you've laid the foundation, the most important work is behind you." I've since learned that this is a principle for all of life: you can never build *anything* larger than the foundation can handle.

The foundation of any building determines both its size and strength, and the same is true of our lives. A life built on a false or faulty foundation will never reach the height that God intends for it to reach. If you skimp on your foundation, you limit your life.

That's why this material is so vitally important. *Foundations* is the biblical basis of a purpose-driven life. You must understand these life-changing truths to enjoy God's purposes for you. This curriculum has been taught, tested, and refined over ten years with thousands of people at Saddleback Church. I've often said that *Foundations* is the most important class in our church.

Why You Need a Biblical Foundation for Life

- *It's the source of personal growth and stability.* So many of the problems in our lives are caused by faulty thinking. That's why Jesus said the truth will set us free and why Colossians 2:7a (CEV) says, *"Plant your roots in Christ and let him be the foundation for your life."*

- *It's the underpinning of a healthy family.* Proverbs 24:3 (TEV) says, *"Homes are built on the foundation of wisdom and understanding."* In a world that is constantly changing, strong families are based on God's unchanging truth.

- *It's the starting point of leadership.* You can never lead people farther than you've gone yourself. Proverbs 16:12b (MSG) says, *"Sound leadership has a moral foundation."*

- *It's the basis for your eternal reward in heaven.* Paul said, *"Whatever we build on that foundation will be tested by fire on the day of judgment . . . We will be rewarded if our building is left standing"* (1 Corinthians 3:12, 14 CEV).

- *God's truth is the only foundation that will last.* The Bible tells us that *"the sound, wholesome teachings of the Lord Jesus Christ . . . are the foundation for a godly life"* (1 Timothy 6:3 NLT), and that *"God's truth stands firm like a foundation stone . . . "* (2 Timothy 2:19 NLT).

Jesus concluded his Sermon on the Mount with a story illustrating this important truth. Two houses were built on different foundations. The house built on sand was destroyed when rain, floods, and wind swept it away. But the house built on the foundation of solid rock remained firm. He concluded, *"Therefore everyone who hears these words of mine and puts them into practice is like a wise man who built his house on the rock"* (Matthew 7:24 NIV). *The Message* paraphrase of this verse shows how important this is: *"These words I speak to you are not incidental additions to your life . . . They are foundational words, words to build a life on."*

I cannot recommend this curriculum more highly to you. It has changed our church, our staff, and thousands of lives. For too long, too many have thought of theology as something that doesn't relate to our everyday lives, but *Foundations* explodes that mold. This study makes it clear that the foundation of what we do and say in each day of our lives is what we believe. I am thrilled that this in-depth, life-changing curriculum is now being made available for everyone to use.

— Rick Warren, author of *The Purpose Driven* ® *Life*

PREFACE

Get ready for a radical statement, a pronouncement sure to make you wonder if we've lost our grip on reality: *There is nothing more exciting than doctrine!*

Track with us for a second on this. Doctrine is the study of what God has to say. What God has to say is always the truth. The truth gives me the right perspective on myself and on the world around me. The right perspective results in decisions of faith and experiences of joy. *That is exciting!*

The objective of *Foundations* is to present the basic truths of the Christian faith in a simple, systematic, and life-changing way. In other words, to teach doctrine. The question is, why? In a world in which people's lives are filled with crying needs, why teach doctrine? Because biblical doctrine has the answer to many of those crying needs! Please don't see this as a clash between needs-oriented and doctrine-oriented teaching. The truth is we need both. We all need to learn how to deal with worry in our lives. One of the keys to dealing with worry is an understanding of the biblical doctrine of the hope of heaven. Couples need to know what the Bible says about how to have a better marriage. They also need a deeper understanding of the doctrine of the Fatherhood of God, giving the assurance of God's love upon which all healthy relationships are built. Parents need to understand the Bible's practical insights for raising kids. They also need an understanding of the sovereignty of God, a certainty of the fact that God is in control, that will carry them through the inevitable ups and downs of being a parent. Doctrinal truth meets our deepest needs.

Welcome to a study that will have a lifelong impact on the way that you look at everything around you and above you and within you. Helping you develop a "Christian worldview" is our goal as the writers of this study. A Christian worldview is the ability to see everything through the filter of God's truth. The time you dedicate to this study will lay a foundation for new perspectives that will have tremendous benefits for the rest of your life. This study will help you to:

- Lessen the stress in everyday life

- See the real potential for growth the Lord has given you

- Increase your sense of security in an often troubling world

- Find new tools for helping others (your friends, your family, your children) find the right perspective on life

- Fall more deeply in love with the Lord

Throughout this study you'll see three types of sidebar sections designed to help you connect with the truths God tells us about himself, ourselves, and this world.

- *A Fresh Word:* One aspect of doctrine that makes people nervous is the "big words." Throughout this study we'll take a fresh look at these words, words like *omnipotent* and *sovereign.*

- *A Closer Look:* We'll take time to expand on a truth or look at it from a different perspective.

- *Living on Purpose:* James 1:22 (NCV) says, *"Do what God's teaching says; when you only listen and do nothing, you are fooling yourselves."* In his book, *The Purpose Driven Life*, Rick Warren identifies God's five purposes for our lives. They are worship, fellowship, discipleship, ministry, and evangelism. We will focus on one of these five purposes in each lesson, and discuss how it relates to the subject of the study. This section is very important, so please be sure to leave time for it.

Here is a brief explanation of the other features of this study guide.

Looking Ahead/Catching Up: You will open each meeting with an opportunity for everyone to check in with each other about how you are doing with the weekly assignments. Accountability is a key to success in this study!

Key Verse: Each week you will find a key verse or Scripture passage for your group to read together. If someone in the group has a different translation, ask them to read it aloud so the group can get a bigger picture of the meaning of the passage.

Video Lesson: There is a video lesson segment for the group to watch together each week. Take notes in the lesson outlines as you watch the video, and be sure to refer back to these notes during your discussion time.

Discovery Questions: Each video segment is complemented by questions for group discussion. Please don't feel pressured to discuss every single question. The material in this study is meant to be your servant, not your master, so there is no reason to rush through the answers. Give everyone ample opportunity to share their thoughts. If you don't get through all of the discovery questions, that's okay.

Prayer Direction: At the end of each session you will find suggestions for your group prayer time. Praying together is one of the greatest privileges of small group life. Please don't take it for granted.

Get ready for God to do incredible things in your life as you begin the adventure of learning more deeply about the most exciting message in the world: the truth about God!

— Tom Holladay and Kay Warren

How to Use This Video Curriculum

Here is a brief explanation of the features on your small group DVD. These features include a *Group Lifter*, four *Video Teaching Sessions* by Tom Holladay and Kay Warren and a short video, *How to Become a Follower of Christ*, by Rick Warren. Here's how they work:

The *Group Lifter* is a brief video introduction by Tom Holladay giving you a sense of the objective and purpose of this *Foundations* study on the Bible. Watch it together as a group at the beginning of your first session.

The *Video Teaching Sessions* provide you with the teaching for each week of the study. Watch these features with your group. After watching the video teaching session, continue in your study by working through the discussion questions and activities in the study guide.

Nothing is more important than the decision you make to accept Jesus Christ as your Lord and Savior. You will have the option to watch a short video presentation, *How to Become a Follower of Jesus Christ*, at the end of Session Two. In this brief video segment, Rick Warren explains the importance of having Christ as the Savior of your life and how you can become part of the family of God. If everyone in your group is already a follower of Christ, or if you feel there is a better time to play this segment, just continue your session by turning to the Discovery Questions in your DVD study guide. You can also select this video presentation separately on the Main Menu of the DVD for viewing at any time.

Follow these simple steps for a successful small group session:

1. Hosts: Watch the video session and write down your answers to the discussion questions in the study guide before your group arrives.

2. Group: Open your group meeting by using the "Looking Ahead" or "Catching Up" section of your lesson.

3. Group: Watch the video teaching lesson and follow along in the outlines in the study guide.

4. Group: Complete the rest of the discussion materials for each session in the study guide.

It's just that simple. Have a great study together!

Session One

1

BUILDING CONFIDENCE
IN THE BIBLE

LOOKING AHEAD

1. What do you hope to get out of this small group study?

2. Share about a time when the Bible had a memorable impact on your life.

Key Verse

[16]All Scripture is God-breathed and is useful for teaching, rebuking, correcting and training in righteousness, [17]so that the man of God may be thoroughly equipped for every good work.

2 Timothy 3:16–17 (NIV)

BIBLE TEACHING
Watch the video lesson now and take notes in your outline on pages 3–8.

Three Important Words, Their Definitions, and Their Implications

1. _____ means that God has chosen to reveal his nature and his will to us through the Bible. The Bible was written so that God could show us what he is like and what he wants us to be like. An understanding of God comes solely through his decision to reveal himself to us.

   "And so I will show my greatness and my holiness, and I will make myself known in the sight of many nations. Then they will know that I am the LORD." (Ezekiel 38:23 NIV)

2. _____ is the process through which God gave us the Bible. God worked in the hearts of human writers to inspire them to write down his words. God's words written through these people are perfect, infallible, and trustworthy.

   All Scripture is inspired by God and is useful to teach us what is true and to make us realize what is wrong in our lives. It straightens us out and teaches us to do what is right. (2 Timothy 3:16 NLT)

3. _____ is the Holy Spirit's work of bringing light to the words of the Bible as we read them. Illumination is the means by which we understand the Bible.

   Then he opened their minds so they could understand the Scriptures. (Luke 24:45 NIV)

How Do We Know the Bible Came from God?

First: The _____ evidence says the Bible is a historical book.

- The number of manuscript copies and the short length of time between the original manuscripts and our first copies of the New Testament

> For the New Testament the evidence is overwhelming. There are 5,366 manuscripts to compare and draw information from, and some of these date from the second or third centuries. To put that in perspective, there are only 643 copies of Homer's *Iliad,* and that is the most famous book of ancient Greece! No one doubts the existence of Julius Caesar's Gallic Wars, but we only have 10 copies of it and the earliest of those was made 1,000 years after it was written. To have such an abundance of copies of the New Testament from dates within 70 years after their writing is amazing.[1]
>
> — Norman L. Geisler

Why didn't God allow us to have the original rather than relying on a number of copies? One possibility: we would have worshiped an old document rather than reading and following his living Word.

- The extreme care with which the Scriptures were copied
- Confirmation of places and dates by archaeology

> Discovery after discovery has established the accuracy of innumerable details, and has brought increased recognition to the value of the Bible as a source of history.[2]
>
> — William Foxwell Albright

---

[1] Norman L. Geisler and Ronald M. Brooks, *When Skeptics Ask: A Handbook of Christian Evidence* (Grand Rapids, Mich.: BakerBooks, A Division of Baker Publishing Group, 1990), 159–60.

[2] William Foxwell Albright, *The Archaeology of Palestine* (Harmondsworth, Middlesex, Great Britain: Pelican Books, 1960), 127.

Second: The _____ *evidence tells us the Bible is a unique book.*

- The majority of the Bible is from eyewitness accounts
- The amazing agreement and consistency throughout the Bible

> The Bible was written over a period of about 1,500 years in various places stretching all the way from Babylon to Rome. The human authors included over 40 persons from various stations of life: kings, peasants, poets, herdsmen, fishermen, scientists, farmers, priests, pastors, tentmakers and governors. It was written in a wilderness, a dungeon, inside palaces and prisons, on lonely islands and in military battles. Yet it speaks with agreement and reliability on hundreds of controversial subjects. Yet it tells one story from beginning to end, God's salvation of man through Jesus Christ. NO PERSON could have possibly conceived of or written such a work![3]
>
> — Josh McDowell

---

[3] Josh McDowell, *Evidence that Demands a Verdict: Historical Evidences for the Christian Faith* (San Bernardino, Calif.: Here's Life Publishers, Inc., 1972), 19–20.

A CLOSER LOOK
What's the Difference?

The Bible is translated from 24,000 copies of the New Testament alone, with millions of people having seen some of these copies. Those copies have been translated by thousands of scholars.	**The Book of Mormon** is translated from a supposed single original that is claimed to have been seen and translated by one man: Joseph Smith (who was not an expert in languages). That original was "taken back." There are no copies of that original.
The Bible was written by more than forty different authors spanning over fifty generations and three continents. It speaks with agreement on all matters of faith and doctrine.	**The Qu'ran** is the writings and record of one man, Muhammad, in one place at one point in history. It differs at many points with the Old and New Testament accounts of history.
The Bible provides God's distinctive solution to man's problem with sin and focuses on God's work in actual, verifiable history.	**Hindu** scriptures claim all roads lead to the same place and focus on stories of things that happened in the "celestial realms."

Third: The _____ evidence says the Bible is a powerful book.

The Bible is the world's bestselling book. Most people know that it was the first major book to be printed on a press (the Gutenburg Bible). The Bible, in whole or in part, has been translated into more than 2,100 languages.

Millions of lives have been changed through the truth in the Bible!

Remember, personal testimony is just one of the four proofs that the Bible is God's book.

Fourth: _____ **said the Bible came from God.**

- Jesus recognized the Holy Spirit as the _____ of the Bible.

> [43] *"Why, then," Jesus asked, "did the Spirit inspire David to call him 'Lord'? David said,* [44] *'The Lord said to my Lord: Sit here at my right side until I put your enemies under your feet.'"*
> (Matthew 22:43–44 GNT)

- Jesus quoted the Bible as _____ .

> *Jesus replied, "You are in error because you do not know the Scriptures or the power of God."* (Matthew 22:29 NIV)

> *He replied, "Blessed rather are those who hear the word of God and obey it."* (Luke 11:28 NIV)

- Jesus proclaimed the Bible's _____ .

> *"I tell you the truth, until heaven and earth disappear, not the smallest letter, not the least stroke of a pen, will by any means disappear from the Law until everything is accomplished."*
> (Matthew 5:18 NIV)

> *". . . Scripture is always true."* (John 10:35 NCV)

- Jesus called the Bible the "_____."

> *"Thus you nullify the word of God by your tradition that you have handed down. And you do many things like that."*
> (Mark 7:13 NIV)

- Jesus believed that people and places in the Bible were
  _____ .

  1) He believed in the _____ (Matthew 22:29; 24:15).

  2) He believed in _____ (Luke 17:26).

  3) He believed in _____ and _____
     (Matthew 19:4).

  4) He believed in _____ and _____
     (Matthew 10:15).

  5) He believed in _____ (Matthew 12:40).

DISCOVERY QUESTIONS

1. Why do you think it is important to know where the Bible came from?

2. Why should we trust the Bible more than any other book? What is so special about it?

3. What is one specific truth God has shown you about himself through the Bible?

4. Share one aspect of this week's study that was especially meaningful to you.

Did You Get It? How has this week's study helped you see that trusting in the Bible as God's Word is more than just a feeling we have?

Share with Someone: Think of a person you can encourage with the truth you learned in this study. Write their name in the space below and pray for God to provide that opportunity this week.

> ## LIVING ON PURPOSE
> ### *Discipleship*
>
> The Bible reveals God to us. How should we respond to this book?
>
> - With awe (Psalm 119:120)
> - With delight (Psalm 1:2)
> - With appreciation (Psalm 119:72)
> - With praise (Psalm 119:62)
> - With joy (Psalm 119:111)
> - With love (Psalm 119:47, 97)
> - With obedience (Deuteronomy 5:32; James 1:22; John 14:15)
>
> Use the verses above in your quiet time before the next session. Take a few moments each day not only to read a verse but also to do what it says. It's amazing how our faith in God's Word is increased through this simple step of telling God how we value his Word.

PRAYER DIRECTION

Take some time as a group to talk about specific prayer requests and to pray for one another.

Session two

2

TRUSTING IN THE
RELIABILITY OF THE BIBLE

CATCHING UP

How did the truth you learned in our last session impact your life this
week? Were you able to share that truth with someone else?

Key Verse

For prophecy never had its origin in the will of man,
but men spoke from God as they were carried along by the Holy Spirit.

2 Peter 1:21 (NIV)

BIBLE TEACHING
Watch the video lesson now and take notes in your outline on pages 13–16.

How Do We Know We Have the Right Books?

The testimony of the _____

• _____ recognized the Old Testament canon. The word "canon" refers to the list of books that are accepted as Scripture.

> *" . . . This is what I told you while I was still with you:*
> *Everything must be fulfilled that is written about me in the*
> *Law of Moses, the Prophets and the Psalms."* (Luke 24:44 NIV)

• _____ recognized part of the New Testament canon.

> *. . . Some things in Paul's letters are hard to understand,*
> *and people who are ignorant and weak in faith explain*
> *these things falsely. They also falsely explain the other*
> *Scriptures, but they are destroying themselves by doing*
> *this.* (2 Peter 3:16 NCV)

• Paul recognized the _____ inspiration of the Old and New Testaments in a single verse.

> *For the Scripture says, "Do not muzzle the ox while it is*
> *treading out the grain," and "The worker deserves his*
> *wages."* (1 Timothy 5:18 NIV)

This is an amazing verse. In it Paul quotes from Deuteronomy 25:4 in the Old Testament and from Luke 10:7 in the New Testament, and calls them both Scripture!

The history of the _____

Books were included in the New Testament on the basis of three things:

1. The authority of an _____

   The New Testament has eyewitness authority. Take the writers of the Gospels, for instance. Matthew was an apostle, Mark wrote down Peter's remembrances, Luke was a friend of Paul, and John was an apostle.

2. The teaching of the _____

3. The confirmation of the _____

   Many people think that the New Testament books were chosen by a council of a few people. That is not true. A council did recognize the books of the New Testament (around 400 AD), but that was after the church had been using these books for 300 years. The council formally recognized the books in response to false teachers who were trying to add books to the Bible.

The _____

> The grass withers and the flowers fall, but the word of our God stands forever. (Isaiah 40:8 NIV)

Our assurance that we have the right books is a matter of faith. God would not have allowed any part of what he had chosen to stand forever to be left out.

What Does It Mean When We Say the Bible Is Inspired?

> ### A FRESH WORD
> #### Inspiration
>
> Inspiration does not mean simply that the writer felt enthusiastic, like Handel composing "The Messiah." Nor does it mean that the writings are necessarily inspiring, like an uplifting poem. As a process, it refers to the writers and the writings being controlled by God. As a product, it refers to the writings only, as documents that are God's message.[1]
>
> — Norman Geisler

Inspiration means God wrote the Bible through

_____ .

> *No prophecy ever came from what a person wanted to say,*
> *but people led by the Holy Spirit spoke words from God.*
> (2 Peter 1:21 NCV)

Inspiration means the Holy Spirit is the _____ .

> *. . . the Scripture had to be fulfilled which the Holy Spirit spoke*
> *long ago through the mouth of David . . .* (Acts 1:16 NIV)

> *The Holy Spirit spoke the truth to your forefathers when he*
> *said through Isaiah the prophet . . .* (Acts 28:25 NIV)

> *Then the Spirit of the LORD came upon me, and he told me to*
> *say . . .* (Ezekiel 11:5 NIV)

---

[1] Norman L. Geisler and Ronald M. Brooks, *When Skeptics Ask: A Handbook of Christian Evidence* (Grand Rapids, Mich.: BakerBooks, A Division of Baker Publishing Group, 1990), 145.

Two important words to understand:

- _____**Inspiration:** God inspired the words, not just the ideas (Matthew 5:18; 22:43–44. Jesus based his argument on the single word "Lord").

- _____**Inspiration:** God inspired all of the Bible, not just part of it (2 Timothy 3:16).

> *As for God, his way is perfect; the word of the LORD is flawless. He is a shield for all who take refuge in him.* (Psalm 18:30 NIV)

> If you believe what you like in the Gospel, and reject what you don't like, it is not the Gospel you believe, but yourself.
>
> — Augustine

Inspiration means God's Word is to be our _____ .

> *How can a young person stay pure? By obeying your word and following its rules.* (Psalm 119:9 NLT)

> *For the word of the LORD holds true, and everything he does is worthy of our trust.* (Psalm 33:4 NLT)

- Understanding inspiration increases my confidence in the Bible.

- The truth behind inspiration is that I can trust his Word above my feelings, values, opinions, and culture.

Whenever there is a conflict between what the Bible says and the way I feel or what I've been taught or the opinions of others or what seems reasonable to me—whenever I have a difference of opinion with the Bible for any reason—the Bible is always right!

DISCOVERY QUESTIONS

1. Why does the inspiration of the Bible give it authority?

2. How committed are you to the following statement? *"Whenever there is a conflict between the way you feel and what the Bible says, or the way you've been taught and what the Bible says, or the opinions of others or what seems reasonable to you—whenever you have a difference of opinion with the Bible for any reason—THE BIBLE IS ALWAYS RIGHT!"* What, if anything, is causing you to doubt its authenticity and authority for your life?

3. What difference does the truth, "the Bible is without error," make in your daily life?

4. Consider your opinions, convictions, values, and goals before you began accepting God's Word as true and reliable. How have you seen the truth of God's Word change these areas of your life?

5. Share a story of a time when you struggled to:

    Trust God's Word above your feelings

    Trust God's Word above the values you've grown up with

    Trust God's Word above your opinions

    Trust God's Word above your culture

6. Share one aspect of this week's study that was especially meaningful to you.

Did You Get It? Which truths from today's study most strongly convince you of the authority and reliability of the Bible? (For help, use your teaching outline.)

Share with Someone: Think of a person you can encourage with the truth you learned this in this study. Write their name in the space below, and pray for God to provide the opportunity this week.

"HOW TO BECOME A FOLLOWER OF JESUS CHRIST"

Have you ever surrendered your life to Jesus Christ? Take a few minutes with your group to watch a brief video by Pastor Rick Warren on how to become part of the family of God. It is included on the menu of this DVD.

> ## LIVING ON PURPOSE
> ### *Worship*
>
> Read Psalm 119 this week. The focus of this psalm is on love for God's Word. There are 176 verses in Psalm 119, so you'll need to read about 26 verses a day.

PRAYER DIRECTION

One of the most refreshing ways we can pray is to pray the truth of the Bible back to God. For this session's prayer time, pray Ephesians 1:3–12 back to God. Here is one way to do this: Have a group member read a verse out loud and pray a prayer of thanksgiving and commitment for the truth in that verse. Then have someone else read the next verse and pray a prayer of thanksgiving and commitment for the truth in that verse.

3

Session three

UNDERSTANDING ILLUMINATION

CATCHING UP

1. How did the truth you learned in our last session impact your life this week? Were you able to share that truth with someone else?

2. What did you learn this last week as you read through Psalm 119?

Key Verse

Your word is a lamp to my feet and a light for my path.

Psalm 119:105 (NIV)

> **BIBLE TEACHING**
> Watch the video lesson now and take notes in your outline on pages 23–26.

Remember the three words:
Revelation, Inspiration, Illumination?

1. **Revelation** has been completed (Hebrews 1:1–2 NIV).

2. **Inspiration** has been completed (1 Peter 1:10–12 NIV).

3. **Illumination** is going on right now.

> *LORD, you have brought light to my life; my God, you light up my darkness.* (Psalm 18:28 NLT)

> *Your word is a lamp to my feet and a light for my path.*
> (Psalm 119:105 NIV)

A FRESH WORD

Illumination

Illumination is the supernatural influence or ministry of the Holy Spirit which enables all who believe in Christ to understand the Scriptures. Picture it this way: with his revelation and by his inspiration, God sent the light of his Word into our world. Through illumination, the blinders are taken off our eyes so that we can see the light that is already there.

Love God's Word _____

> How I love your teachings! I think about them all day long.
> (Psalm 119:97 NCV)

> Truly, I love your commands more than gold, even the
> finest gold. (Psalm 119:127 NLT)

> ³And if you call out for insight and cry aloud for
> understanding, ⁴and if you look for it as for silver
> and search for it as for hidden treasure, ⁵then you
> will understand the fear of the LORD and find
> the knowledge of God. ⁶For the LORD gives wisdom,
> and from his mouth come knowledge and understanding.
> (Proverbs 2:3–6 NIV)

How does the Bible picture its potential for changing our lives?

- _____

> For you have been born again, not of perishable seed, but of
> imperishable, through the living and enduring word of God.
> (1 Peter 1:23 NIV)

- _____

> Take the helmet of salvation and the sword of the Spirit, which
> is the word of God. (Ephesians 6:17 NIV)

> For the word of God is living and active. Sharper than any
> double-edged sword, it penetrates even to dividing soul and
> spirit, joints and marrow; it judges the thoughts and attitudes
> of the heart. (Hebrews 4:12 NIV)

In Ephesians the sword is in our hand, defending against the enemy. In Hebrews, the sword is in God's hands, penetrating and deeply impacting our lives.

- _____

When your words came, I ate them; they were my joy and my heart's delight, for I bear your name, O LORD God Almighty. (Jeremiah 15:16 NIV)

Jesus answered, "It is written: 'Man does not live on bread alone, but on every word that comes from the mouth of God.'" (Matthew 4:4 NIV)

Like newborn babies, crave pure spiritual milk, so that by it you may grow up in your salvation. (1 Peter 2:2 NIV)

- _____

"Is not my word like fire," declares the LORD, "and like a hammer that breaks a rock in pieces?" (Jeremiah 23:29 NIV)

- _____

[23]Anyone who listens to the word but does not do what it says is like a man who looks at his face in a mirror [24]and, after looking at himself, goes away and immediately forgets what he looks like. [25]But the man who looks intently into the perfect law that gives freedom, and continues to do this, not forgetting what he has heard, but doing it—he will be blessed in what he does. (James 1:23–25 NIV)

Understand God's Word _____

Two truths about every believer in Christ:

1. The Holy Spirit makes me _____ to understand the Bible.

    > *[12]And God has actually given us his Spirit (not the world's spirit) so we can know the wonderful things God has freely given us. [13]When we tell you this, we do not use words of human wisdom. We speak words given to us by the Spirit, using the Spirit's words to explain spiritual truths. [14]But people who aren't Christians can't understand these truths from God's Spirit. It all sounds foolish to them because only those who have the Spirit can understand what the Spirit means. [15]We who have the Spirit understand these things, but others can't understand us at all.* (1 Corinthians 2:12–15 NLT)

    > *"But when he, the Spirit of truth, comes, he will guide you into all truth."* (John 16:13a NIV)

2. The Holy Spirit makes me _____ for understanding the Bible.

    > *[20]But you have an anointing from the Holy One, and all of you know the truth . . . [27]As for you, the anointing you received from him remains in you, and you do not need anyone to teach you. But as his anointing teaches you about all things and as that anointing is real, not counterfeit—just as it has taught you, remain in him.* (1 John 2:20, 27 NIV)

DISCOVERY QUESTIONS

1. Share with the group how you would complete one of the following statements:

The Bible was like a seed to me when . . .

The Bible was like a sword to me when . . .

The Bible was like food to me when . . .

The Bible was like a hammer to me when . . .

The Bible was like a fire to me when . . .

The Bible was like a mirror to me when . . .

2. The Holy Spirit gives us understanding of God's Word individually. The Bible says in 1 John 2:27 (NIV) that *"you do not need anyone to teach you."* Yet the New Testament talks about, and even tells us to honor, the gifts of teaching and preaching. Why do we need teachers? How do these two truths fit together?

3. Share one aspect of this week's study that was especially meaningful to you.

Did You Get It? How has this week's study helped you understand the Bible's potential for changing your life?

Share with Someone: Think of a person you can encourage with the truth you learned in this study. Write their name in the space below and pray for God to provide that opportunity this week.

LIVING ON PURPOSE
Evangelism
Who do you know who is missing out on the awesome benefits that the truth of God's Word brings into our lives? Write their name down, and pray for them this week.

PRAYER DIRECTION

Take some time as a group to talk about specific prayer requests and to pray for one another.

NOTES

Session four

4

HANDLING THE BIBLE
RESPONSIBLY

Catching Up

1. How did the truth you learned in our last session impact your life this week? Were you able to share that truth with someone else?

2. Are you praying for someone to understand the truth of the Bible more clearly? Share his or her name with the group and pray for that person together.

Key Verse

Be diligent to present yourself approved to God as a workman who does not need to be ashamed, accurately handling the word of truth.

2 Timothy 2:15 (NASB)

> **BIBLE TEACHING**
> Watch the video lesson now and take notes in your outline on pages 33–35.

Handle God's Word _____

> *Be diligent to present yourself approved to God as a workman who does not need to be ashamed, accurately handling the word of truth.* (2 Timothy 2:15 NASB)

Seven Rules of Bible Study

Rule 1: Faith and the Holy Spirit are necessary for proper

_____ .

Rule 2: The Bible _____ .

    Application: Learn to do cross-reference studies.

Rule 3: Understand the Old Testament in light of the _____

_____ .

    Example: The Old Testament Law

Rule 4: Understand unclear passages in the light of _____ passages.

    Example: Now if there is no resurrection, what will those do who are baptized for the dead? (1 Corinthians 15:29a NIV).

Rule 5: Understand words and verses in the light of their

_____ .

> **_Example:_** _"Take life easy; eat, drink and be merry"_
> (Luke 12:19b NIV).

Rule 6: Understand historical passages in the light of _____ passages.

> **_Examples:_** _The king must not take many wives for himself, because they will lead him away from the LORD_
> (Deuteronomy 17:17a NLT).
>
> _Very early in the morning, while it was still dark, Jesus got up, left the house and went off to a solitary place, where he prayed_
> (Mark 1:35 NIV).

Rule 7: Understand personal experience in the light of

_____ .

> **_Example:_** _Owe nothing to anyone . . ._ (Romans 13:8 NASB).

Study God's Word _____

How do you decide to study God's Word as a lifetime commitment?

1. _____ before the Lord to trust in and commit to the truth of his Word.

> [15]*Be diligent in these matters; give yourself wholly to them, so that everyone may see your progress.* [16a]*Watch your life and doctrine closely. Persevere in them* . . . (1 Timothy 4:15–16a NIV)

2. _____ by examining God's Word for answers.

> . . . *they* [the Bereans] *received the message with great eagerness and examined the Scriptures every day to see if what Paul said was true.* (Acts 17:11 NIV)

3. _____ what you're learning from God's Word.

> *Let the word of Christ dwell in you richly as you teach and admonish one another with all wisdom* . . . (Colossians 3:16 NIV)

4. _____ on what you learn as you study the Bible.

> *Do not merely listen to the word, and so deceive yourselves. Do what it says.* (James 1:22 NIV)

DISCOVERY QUESTIONS

1. Which of the seven rules of Bible study is most helpful to you?

2. Which of the truths we have studied in the last four weeks has most convinced you of the wonder and reliability of the Bible?

3. Identify any specific ways in which your life has been changed by this four-week study of God's Word.

4. When has your small group encouraged you with God's Word as you worked through a personal struggle or decision?

Did You Get It? How has this week's study strengthened your confidence in your God-given ability to understand the Bible for yourself?

Share with Someone: Think of a person you can encourage with the truth you learned in this study. Write their name in the space below and pray for God to provide that opportunity this week?

LIVING ON PURPOSE
Fellowship
Get together with your spiritual partner this week—possibly for lunch or coffee—to talk about this study on the Bible. Share what was meaningful to you, and discuss any questions you may continue to have about the role of the Bible in your life.

PRAYER DIRECTION

Pray prayers of praise together, thanking God for how the truth of the Bible has impacted your life and the lives of others you know and love.

NOTES

SmaLL Group Resources

HELPS FOR HOSTS

Top Ten Ideas for New Hosts

Congratulations! As the host of your small group, you have responded to the call to help shepherd Jesus' flock. Few other tasks in the family of God surpass the contribution you will be making.

As you prepare to facilitate your group, whether it is one session or the entire series, here are a few thoughts to keep in mind. We encourage you to read and review these tips with each new discussion host before he or she leads.

Remember you are not alone. God knows everything about you, and he knew you would be asked to facilitate your group. Even though you may not feel ready, this is common for all good hosts. God promises, *"I will never leave you; I will never abandon you"* (Hebrews 13:5 TEV). Whether you are facilitating for one evening, several weeks, or a lifetime, you will be blessed as you serve.

1. **Don't try to do it alone.** Pray right now for God to help you build a healthy team. If you can enlist a cohost to help you shepherd the group, you will find your experience much richer. This is your chance to involve as many people as you can in building a healthy group. All you have to do is ask people to help. You'll be surprised at the response.

2. **Be friendly and be yourself.** God wants to use your unique gifts and temperament. Be sure to greet people at the door with a big smile . . . this can set the mood for the whole gathering. Remember, they are taking as big a step to show up at your house as you are to lead this group! Don't try to do things exactly like another host; do them in a way that fits you. Admit when you don't have an answer and apologize when you make a mistake. Your group will love you for it and you'll sleep better at night.

3. **Prepare for your meeting ahead of time.** Review the session and write down your responses to each question. Pay special attention to exercises that ask group members to do something other than engage in discussion. These exercises will help your group live what the Bible teaches, not just talk about it. Be sure you understand how an exercise works. If the exercise employs one of the items in the Small Group Resources section (such as the Group Guidelines), be sure to look over that item so you'll know how it works.

4. **Pray for your group members by name.** Before you begin your session, take a few moments and pray for each member by name. You may want to review the prayer list at least once a week. Ask God to use your time together to touch the heart of every person in your group. Expect God to lead you to whomever he wants you to encourage or challenge in a special way. If you listen, God will surely lead.

5. **When you ask a question, be patient.** Someone will eventually respond. Sometimes people need a moment or two of silence to think about the question. If silence doesn't bother you, it won't bother anyone else. After someone responds, affirm the response with a simple "thanks" or "great answer." Then ask, "How about somebody else?" or "Would someone who hasn't shared like to add anything?" Be sensitive to new people or reluctant members who aren't ready to say, pray, or do anything. If you give them a safe setting, they will blossom over time. If someone in your group is a "wallflower" who sits silently through every session, consider talking to them privately and encouraging them to participate. Let them know how important they are to you—that they are loved and appreciated—and that the group would value their input. Remember, still water often runs deep.

6. **Provide transitions between questions.** Ask if anyone would like to read the paragraph or Bible passage. Don't call on anyone, but ask for a volunteer, and then be patient until someone begins. Be sure to thank the person who reads aloud.

7. **Break into smaller groups occasionally.** With a greater opportunity to talk in a small circle, people will connect more with the study, apply more quickly what they're learning, and ultimately get more out of their small group experience. A small circle also encourages a quiet person to participate and tends to minimize the effects of a more vocal or dominant member.

8. **Small circles are also helpful during prayer time.** People who are unaccustomed to praying aloud will feel more comfortable trying it with just two or three others. Also, prayer requests won't take as much time, so circles will have more time to actually pray. When you gather back with the whole group, you can have one person from each circle briefly update everyone on the prayer requests from their subgroups. The other great aspect of subgrouping is that it fosters leadership development. As you ask people in the group to facilitate discussion or to lead a prayer circle, it gives them a small leadership step that can build their confidence.

9. **Rotate facilitators occasionally.** You may be perfectly capable of hosting each time, but you will help others grow in their faith and gifts if you give them opportunities to host the group.

10. **One final challenge (for new or first-time hosts).** Before your first opportunity to lead, look up each of the six passages that follow. Read each one as a devotional exercise to help prepare you with a shepherd's heart. Trust us on this one. If you do this, you will be more than ready for your first meeting.

Matthew 9:36–38 (NIV)

36When Jesus saw the crowds, he had compassion on them, because they were harassed and helpless, like sheep without a shepherd. 37Then he said to his disciples, "The harvest is plentiful but the workers are few. 38Ask the Lord of the harvest, therefore, to send out workers into his harvest field."

John 10:14–15 (NIV)

14I am the good shepherd; I know my sheep and my sheep know me—15just as the Father knows me and I know the Father—and I lay down my life for the sheep.

1 Peter 5:2–4 (NIV)

2Be shepherds of God's flock that is under your care, serving as overseers—not because you must, but because you are willing, as God wants you to be; 3not greedy for money, but eager to serve; not lording it over those entrusted to you, but being examples to the flock. 4And when the Chief Shepherd appears, you will receive the crown of glory that will never fade away.

Philippians 2:1–5 (NIV)

1If you have any encouragement from being united with Christ, if any comfort from his love, if any fellowship with the Spirit, if any tenderness and compassion, 2then make my joy complete by being like-minded, having the same love, being one in spirit and purpose. 3Do nothing out of selfish ambition or vain conceit, but in humility consider others better than yourselves. 4Each of you should look not only to your own interests, but also to the interests of others. 5Your attitude should be the same as that of Jesus Christ.

Hebrews 10:23–25 (NIV)

23Let us hold unswervingly to the hope we profess, for he who promised is faithful. 24And let us consider how we may spur one another on toward love and good deeds. 25Let us not give up meeting together, as some are in the habit of doing, but let us encourage one another—and all the more as you see the Day approaching.

1 Thessalonians 2:7–8, 11–12 (NIV)

7. . . but we were gentle among you, like a mother caring for her little children. 8We loved you so much that we were delighted to share with you not only the gospel of God but our lives as well, because you had become so dear to us. . . . 11For you know that we dealt with each of you as a father deals with his own children, 12encouraging, comforting and urging you to live lives worthy of God, who calls you into his kingdom and glory.

FREQUENTLY ASKED QUESTIONS

How long will this group meet?

This volume of *Foundations: The Bible* is four sessions long. We encourage your group to add a fifth session for a celebration. In your final session, each group member may decide if he or she desires to continue on for another study. At that time you may also want to do some informal evaluation, discuss your Group Guidelines, and decide which study you want to do next. We recommend you visit our website at **www.saddlebackresources.com** for more video-based small group studies.

Who is the host?

The host is the person who coordinates and facilitates your group meetings. In addition to a host, we encourage you to select one or more group members to lead your group discussions. Several other responsibilities can be rotated, including refreshments, prayer requests, worship, or keeping up with those who miss a meeting. Shared ownership in the group helps everybody grow.

Where do we find new group members?

Recruiting new members can be a challenge for groups, especially new groups with just a few people, or existing groups that lose a few people along the way. We encourage you to use the *Circles of Life* diagram on page 48 of this DVD study guide to brainstorm a list of people from your workplace, church, school, neighborhood, family, and so on. Then pray for the people on each member's list. Allow each member to invite several people from their list. Some groups fear that newcomers will interrupt the intimacy that members have built over time. However, groups that welcome newcomers generally gain strength with the infusion of new blood. Remember, the next person you add just might become a friend for eternity. Logistically, groups find different ways to add members. Some groups remain permanently open, while others choose to open periodically, such as at the beginning or end of a study. If your group becomes too large for easy, face-to-face conversations, you can subgroup, forming a second discussion group in another room.

How do we handle the child care needs in our group?

Child care needs must be handled very carefully. This is a sensitive issue. We suggest you seek creative solutions as a group. One common solution is to have the adults meet in the living room and share the cost of a babysitter (or two) who can be with the kids in another part of the house. Another popular option is to have one home for the kids and a second home (close by) for the adults. If desired, the adults could rotate the responsibility of providing a lesson for the kids. This last option is great with school-age kids and can be a huge blessing to families.

GROUP GUIDELINES

It's a good idea for every group to put words to their shared values, expectations, and commitments. Such guidelines will help you avoid unspoken agendas and unmet expectations. We recommend you discuss your guidelines during Session One in order to lay the foundation for a healthy group experience. Feel free to modify anything that does not work for your group.

We agree to the following values:

Clear Purpose To grow healthy spiritual lives by building a healthy small group community

Group Attendance To give priority to the group meeting (call if I am absent or late)

Safe Environment To create a safe place where people can be heard and feel loved (no quick answers, snap judgments, or simple fixes)

Be Confidential To keep anything that is shared strictly confidential and within the group

Conflict Resolution To avoid gossip and to immediately resolve any concerns by following the principles of Matthew 18:15–17

Spiritual Health To give group members permission to speak into my life and help me live a healthy, balanced spiritual life that is pleasing to God

Limit Our Freedom To limit our freedom by not serving or consuming alcohol during small group meetings or events so as to avoid causing a weaker brother or sister to stumble (1 Corinthians 8:1–13; Romans 14:19–21)

Welcome Newcomers   To invite friends who might benefit from this study and warmly welcome newcomers

Building Relationships   To get to know the other members of the group and pray for them regularly

Other   _____

We have also discussed and agreed on the following items:

Child Care

_____

_____

Starting Time

_____

Ending Time

_____

If you haven't already done so, take a few minutes to fill out the *Small Group Calendar* on page 52.

CIRCLES OF LIFE—SMALL GROUP CONNECTIONS

Discover who you can connect in community

Use this chart to help carry out one of the values in the Group Guidelines to "Welcome Newcomers."

"Follow me, and I will make you fishers of men." (Matthew 4:19 KJV)

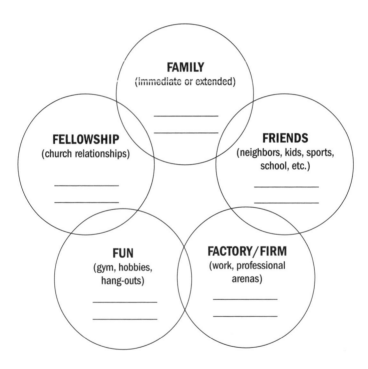

Follow this simple three-step process:

1. List 1–2 people in each circle.

2. Prayerfully select one person or couple from your list and tell your group about them.

3. Give them a call and invite them to your next meeting. Over 50 percent of those invited to a small group say, "Yes!"

SMALL GROUP PRAYER AND PRAISE REPORT

This is a place where you can write each other's requests for prayer.
You can also make a note when God answers a prayer. Pray for each
other's requests. If you're new to group prayer, it's okay to pray silently
or to pray by using just one sentence: "God, please help

_____ to _____ ."

DATE	PERSON	PRAYER REQUEST	PRAISE REPORT

SMALL GROUP PRAYER AND PRAISE REPORT

DATE	PERSON	PRAYER REQUEST	PRAISE REPORT

SMALL GROUP PRAYER AND PRAISE REPORT

DATE	PERSON	PRAYER REQUEST	PRAISE REPORT

SMALL GROUP CALENDAR

Healthy groups share responsibilities and group ownership. It might take some time for this to develop. Shared ownership ensures that responsibility for the group doesn't fall to one person. Use the calendar to keep track of social events, mission projects, birthdays, or days off. Complete this calendar at your first or second meeting. Planning ahead will increase attendance and shared ownership.

DATE	LESSON	LOCATION	FACILITATOR	SNACK OR MEAL
5/4	Session 2	Chris and Andrea	Jim Brown	Phil and Karen

ANSWER KEY

Session One:
Building Confidence in the Bible

1. Revelation
2. Inspiration
3. Illumination

First: The external evidence says the Bible is a historical book.

Second: The internal evidence tell us the Bible is a unique book.

Third: The personal evidence says the Bible is a powerful book.

Fourth: Jesus said the Bible came from God.

- Jesus recognized the Holy Spirit as the author of the Bible.
- Jesus quoted the Bible as authoritative.
- Jesus proclaimed the Bible's uniqueness.
- Jesus called the Bible the "Word of God."
- Jesus believed that people and places in the Bible were real.

  1) He believed in the prophets.
  2) He believed in Noah.
  3) He believed in Adam and Eve.
  4) He believed in Sodom and Gomorrah.
  5) He believed in Jonah.

Session Two:
Trusting in the Reliability
of the Bible

The testimony of the Bible itself

- Jesus recognized the Old Testament canon.
- Peter recognized part of the New Testament canon.
- Paul recognized the equal inspiration of the Old and New Testaments in a single verse.

The history of the church
1. The authority of an apostle
2. The teaching of the truth
3. The confirmation of the church

The power of God

Inspiration means God wrote the Bible through people.

Inspiration means the Holy Spirit is the author.

- Verbal Inspiration
- Plenary Inspiration

Inspiration means God's Word is to be our final authority.

Session Three:
Understanding Illumination

Love God's Word Deeply
- Seed
- Sword
- Food
- Hammer and Fire
- Mirror

Understand God's Word Spiritually
1. The Holy Spirit makes me able to understand the Bible.
2. The Holy Spirit makes me responsible for understanding the Bible.

Session Four:
Handling the Bible Responsibly

Handle God's Word Accurately

Rule 1: Faith and the Holy Spirit are necessary for proper interpretation.

Rule 2: The Bible interprets itself.

Rule 3: Understand the Old Testament in light of the New Testament.

Rule 4: Understand unclear passages in the light of clear passages.

Rule 5: Understand words and verses in the light of their context.

Rule 6: Understand historical passages in the light of doctrinal passages.

Rule 7: Understand personal experience in the light of Scripture.

Study God's Word Diligently

1. Vow before the Lord to trust in and commit to the truth of his Word.

2. Cultivate eagerness by examining God's Word for answers.

3. Tell others what you're learning from God's Word.

4. Act on what you learn as you study the Bible.

NOTES

KEY VERSES

One of the most effective ways to drive deeply into our lives the principles we are learning in this series is to memorize key Scriptures. For many, memorization is a new concept or one that has been difficult in the past. We encourage you to stretch yourself and try to memorize these four key verses. If possible, memorize these as a group and make them part of your group time. You may cut these apart and carry them in your wallet.

I have hidden your word in my heart that I might not sin against you.

Psalm 119:11 (NIV)

Session One

[16]All Scripture is God-breathed and is useful for teaching, rebuking, correcting, and training in righteousness, [17]so that the man of God may be thoroughly equipped for every good work.

2 Timothy 3:16–17 (NIV)

Session Two

For prophecy never had its origin in the will of man, but men spoke from God as they were carried along by the Holy Spirit.

2 Peter 1:21 (NIV)

Session Three

Your word is a lamp to my feet and a light for my path.

Psalm 119:105 (NIV)

Session Four

Be diligent to present yourself approved to God as a workman who does not need to be ashamed, accurately handling the word of truth.

2 Timothy 2:15 (NASB)

NOTES

We value your thoughts about what you've just read.
Please share them with us. You'll find contact information
in the back of this book.

The Purpose Driven® Life
A six-session video-based study for groups or individuals

Embark on a journey of discovery with this video-based study taught by Rick Warren. In it you will discover the answer to life's most fundamental question: "What on earth am I here for?"

And here's a clue to the answer: It's not about you . . . You were created by God and for God, and until you understand that, life will never make sense. It is only in God that we discover our origin, our identity, our meaning, our purpose, our significance, and our destiny."

Whether you experience this adventure with a small group or on your own, this six-session, video-based study will change your life.

DVD Study Guide: 978-0-310-27866-5
DVD: 978-0-310-27864-1

Be sure to combine this study with your reading of the best-selling book, *The Purpose Driven® Life*, to give you or your small group the opportunity to discuss the implications and applications of living the life God created you to live.

Hardcover, Jacketed: 978-0-310-20571-5
Softcover: 978-0-310-27699-9

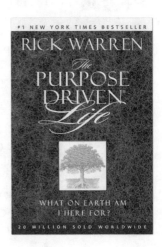

Pick up a copy today at your favorite bookstore!

ZONDERVAN®
.com

Foundations: 11 Core Truths to Build Your Life On

Taught by Tom Holladay and Kay Warren

Foundations is a series of 11 four-week video studies covering the most important, foundational doctrines of the Christian faith. Study topics include:

The Bible—This study focuses on where the Bible came from, why it can be trusted, and how it can change your life.

DVD Study Guide: 978-0-310-27670-8
DVD: 978-0-310-27669-2

God—This study focuses not just on facts about God, but on how to know God himself in a more powerful and personal way.

DVD Study Guide: 978-0-310-27672-2
DVD: 978-0-310-27671-5

Jesus—As we look at what the Bible says about the person of Christ, we do so as people who are developing a lifelong relationship with Jesus.

DVD Study Guide: 978-0-310-27674-6
DVD: 978-0-310-27673-9

The Holy Spirit—This study focuses on the person, the presence, and the power of the Holy Spirit, and how you can be filled with the Holy Spirit on a daily basis.

DVD Study Guide: 978-0-310-27676-0
DVD: 978-0-310-27675-3

Creation—Each of us was personally created by a loving God. This study does not shy away from the great scientific and theological arguments that surround the creation/evolution debate. However, you will find the goal of this study is deepening your awareness of God as your Creator.

DVD Study Guide: 978-0-310-27678-4
DVD: 978-0-310-27677-7

Pick up a copy today at your favorite bookstore!

ZONDERVAN®
.com

Salvation—This study focuses on God's solution to man's need for salvation, what Jesus Christ did for us on the cross, and the assurance and security of God's love and provision for eternity.

DVD Study Guide: 978-0-310-27682-1
DVD: 978-0-310-27679-1

Sanctification—This study focuses on the two natures of the Christian. We'll see the difference between grace and law, and how these two things work in our lives.

DVD Study Guide: 978-0-310-27684-5
DVD: 978-0-310-27683-8

Good and Evil—Why do bad things happen to good people? Through this study we'll see how and why God continues to allow evil to exist. The ultimate goal is to build up our faith and relationship with God as we wrestle with these difficult questions.

DVD Study Guide: 978-0-310-27687-6
DVD: 978-0-310-27686-9

The Afterlife—The Bible does not answer all the questions we have about what happens to us after we die; however, this study deals with what the Bible does tell us. This important study gives us hope and helps us move from a focus on the here and now to a focus on eternity.

DVD Study Guide: 978-0-310-27689-0
DVD: 978-0-310-27688-3

The Church—This study focuses on the birth of the church, the nature of the church, and the mission of the church.

DVD Study Guide: 978-0-310-27692-0
DVD: 978-0-310-27691-3

The Second Coming—This study addresses both the hope and the uncertainties surrounding the second coming of Jesus Christ.

DVD Study Guide: 978-0-310-27695-1
DVD: 978-0-310-27693-7

Pick up a copy today at your favorite bookstore!

Celebrate Recovery, Updated Curriculum Kit

This kit will provide your church with the tools necessary to start a successful Celebrate Recovery program. *Kit includes:*

- Introductory Guide for Leaders DVD
- Leader's Guide
- 4 Participant's Guides (one of each guide)
- CD-ROM with 25 lessons
- CD-ROM with sermon transcripts
- 4-volume audio CD sermon series

Curriculum Kit: 978-0-310-26847-5

Participant's Guide 4-pack

The Celebrate Recovery Participant's Guide 4-pack is a convenient resource when you're just getting started or if you need replacement guides for your program.

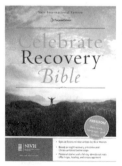

Celebrate Recovery Bible

With features based on eight principles Jesus voiced in his Sermon on the Mount, the new Celebrate Recovery bible offers hope, encouragement, and empowerment for those struggling with the circumstances of their livesand the habits they are trying to control.

Hardcover: 978-0-310-92849-2
Softcover: 978-0-310-93810-1

Pick up a copy today at your favorite bookstore!

ZONDERVAN®
.com

Stepping Out of Denial into God's Grace

Participant's Guide 1 introduces the eight principles of recovery based on Jesus' words in the Beatitudes, and focuses on principles 1–3. Participants learn about denial, hope, sanity, and more.

Getting Right with God, Yourself, and Others

Participant's Guide 3 covers principles 5–7 based on Jesus' words in the Beatitudes. With courage and support from their fellow participants, people seeking recovery will find victory, forgiveness, and grace.

Taking an Honest and Spiritual Inventory

Participant's Guide 2 focuses on the fourth principle based on Jesus' words in the Beatitudes and builds on the Scripture, *"Happy are the pure in heart."* (Matthew 5:8) The participant will learn an invaluable principle for recovery and also take an in-depth spiritual inventory.

Growing in Christ While Helping Others

Participant's Guide 4 walks through the final steps of the eight recovery principles based on Jesus' words in the Beatitudes. In this final phase, participants learn to move forward in newfound freedom in Christ, learning how to give back to others. There's even a practical lesson called "Seven reasons we get stuck in our recoveries."

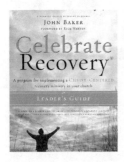

Leader's Guide

The Celebrate Recovery Leader's Guide gives you everything you need to facilitate your preparation time. Virtually walking you through every meeting, the Leader's Guide is a must-have for every leader on your Celebrate Recovery ministry team.

Pick up a copy today at your favorite bookstore!

Wide Angle:
Framing Your Worldview

Christianity is much more than a religion. It is a worldview—a way of seeing all of life and the world around you. Your worldview impacts virtually every decision you make in life: moral decisions, relational decisions, financial decisions—everything. How you see the world determines how you face the world.

In this brand new study, Rick Warren and Chuck Colson discuss such key issues as moral relativism, tolerance, terrorism, creationism vs. Darwinism, sin and suffering. They explore in depth the Christian worldview as it relates to the most important questions in life:

- Why does it matter what I believe?
- How do I know what's true?
- Where do I come from?
- Why is the world so messed up?
- Is there a solution?
- What is my purpose in life?

This study is as deep as it is wide, addressing vitally important topics for every follower of Christ.

Rick Warren

Chuck Colson

DVD Study Guide: 978-1-4228-0083-6
DVD: 978-1-4228-0082-9

The Way of a Worshiper

The pursuit of God is the chase of a lifetime—in fact, it's been going on since the day you were born. The question is: Have you been the hunter or the prey?

This small group study is not about music. It's not even about going to church. It's about living your life as an offering of worship to God. It's about tapping into the source of power to live the Christian life. And it's about discovering the secret to friendship with God.

In these four video sessions, Buddy Owens helps you unpack the meaning of worship. Through his very practical, engaging, and at times surprising insights, Buddy shares truths from Scripture and from life that will help you understand in a new and deeper way just what it means to be a worshiper.

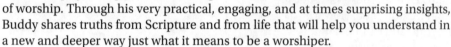

God is looking for worshipers. His invitation to friendship is open and genuine. Will you take him up on his offer? Will you give yourself to him in worship? Then come walk *The Way of a Worshiper* and discover the secret to friendship with God.

DVD Study Guide: 978-1-4228-0096-6
DVD: 978-1-4228-0095-9

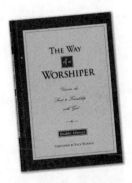

THE WAY of a WORSHIPER

Your study of this material will be greatly enhanced by reading the book, *The Way of a Worshiper: Discover the Secret to Friendship with God.*

Managing Our Finances God's Way

Did you know that there are over 2,350 verses in the Bible about money? Did you know that nearly half of Jesus' parables are about possessions? The Bible is packed with wise counsel about your financial life. In fact, Jesus had more to say about money than about heaven and hell combined.

Introducing a new video-based small group study that will inspire you to live debt free! Created by Saddleback Church and Crown Financial Ministries, learn what the Bible has to say about our finances from Rick Warren, Chip Ingram, Ron Blue, Howard Dayton, and Chuck Bentley as they address important topics like:

- God's Solution to Debt
- Saving and Investing
- Plan Your Spending
- Giving as an Act of Worship
- Enjoy What God Has Given You

Study includes:

- DVD with seven 20-minute lessons

- Workbook with seven lessons

- Resource CD with digital version of all worksheets that perform calculations automatically

- Contact information for help with answering questions

- Resources for keeping financial plans on track and making them lifelong habits

DVD Study Guide: 978-1-4228-0083-6
DVD: 978-1-4228-0082-9

> **NOTE:** PARTICIPANTS DO NOT SHARE PERSONAL FINANCIAL INFORMATION WITH EACH OTHER.

Share Your Thoughts

With the Author: Your comments will be forwarded to
the author when you send them to *zauthor@zondervan.com*.

With Zondervan: Submit your review of this book
by writing to *zreview@zondervan.com*.

Free Online Resources at
www.zondervan.com/hello

 Zondervan AuthorTracker: Be notified whenever your
favorite authors publish new books, go on tour, or post
an update about what's happening in their lives.

 Daily Bible Verses and Devotions: Enrich your life
with daily Bible verses or devotions that help you start
every morning focused on God.

 Free Email Publications: Sign up for newsletters on
fiction, Christian living, church ministry, parenting, and
more.

 Zondervan Bible Search: Find and compare
Bible passages in a variety of translations at
www.zondervanbiblesearch.com.

 Other Benefits: Register yourself to receive online
benefits like coupons and special offers, or to participate
in research.